Let's Draw!
Cute and Easy Images

indilop@vistacolorspublishing.com
All Rights Reserved 2024

Thank You for Choosing us

We will Appreciate your Feedback on Amazon

This Book Belongs To

How to use this book

To get started, gather a pencil and an eraser. Feel free to use pens, markers, or any other drawing tool you prefer.

Begin by lightly sketching, allowing for easy erasing in case of mistakes.

Progress by following the step-by-step instructions indicated by the arrows.

If you find yourself struggling, reference the final drawing for guidance.

Once you've finished your drawing, feel free to add color however desired.

Whale

Milk tea

Start

Ta-da!

Your Drawing

Fish

Start

Ta-da!

Your Drawing

Boat

Mushrom

Your Drawing

Penguin

Start

Ta-da!

Your Drawing

Pot

Your Drawing

Boat

Start

Ta-da!

Your Drawing

Santa

Your Drawing

Cactus

Start

Ta-da!

Your Drawing

Giraffe

Start

Ta-da!

Llama

Clock

Your Drawing

Lion

Spider

Your Drawing

Hippo

Start

Ta-da!

Your Drawing

House

Your Drawing

Potion

Start

Ta-da!

Burger

Record Player

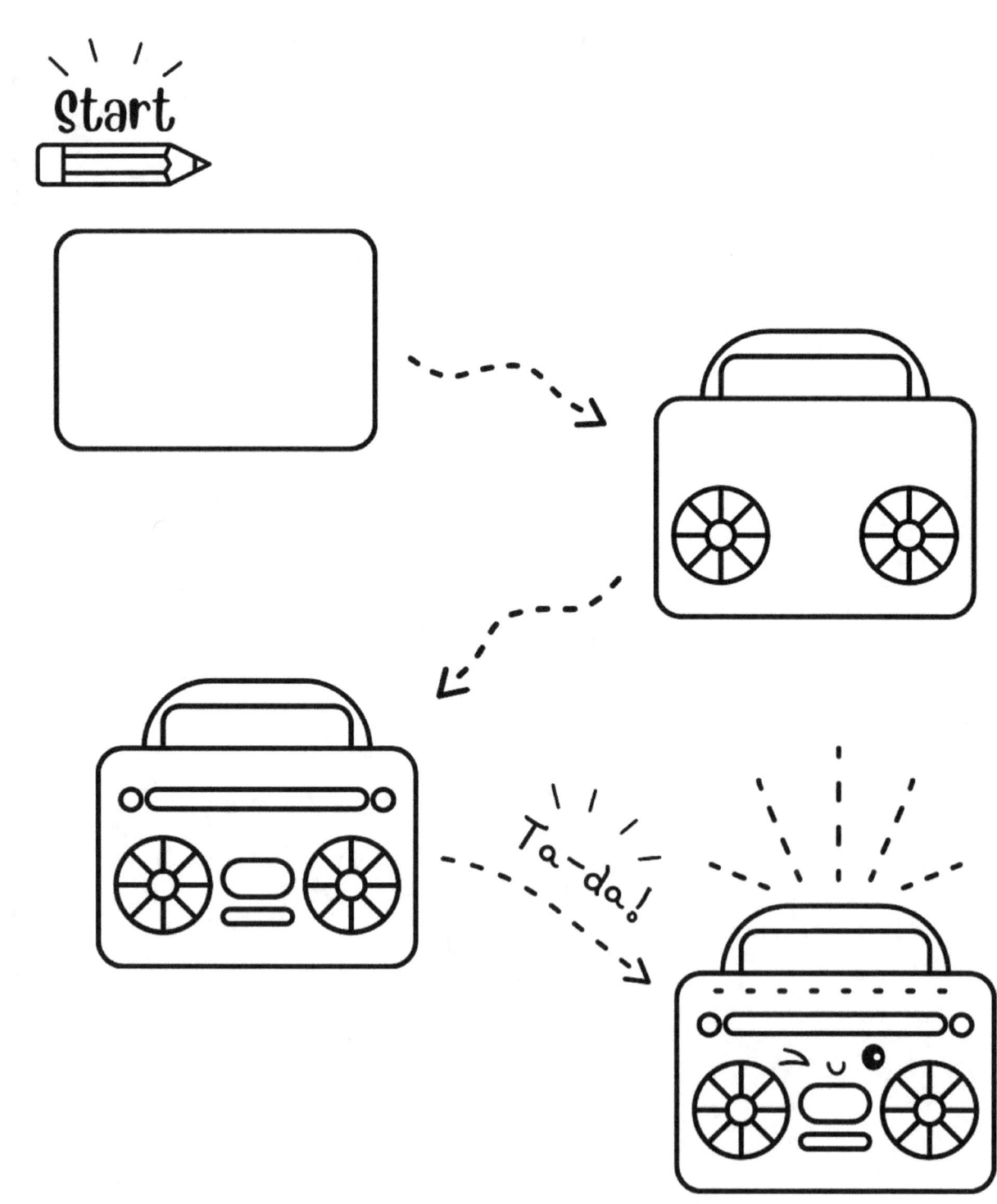

Ship

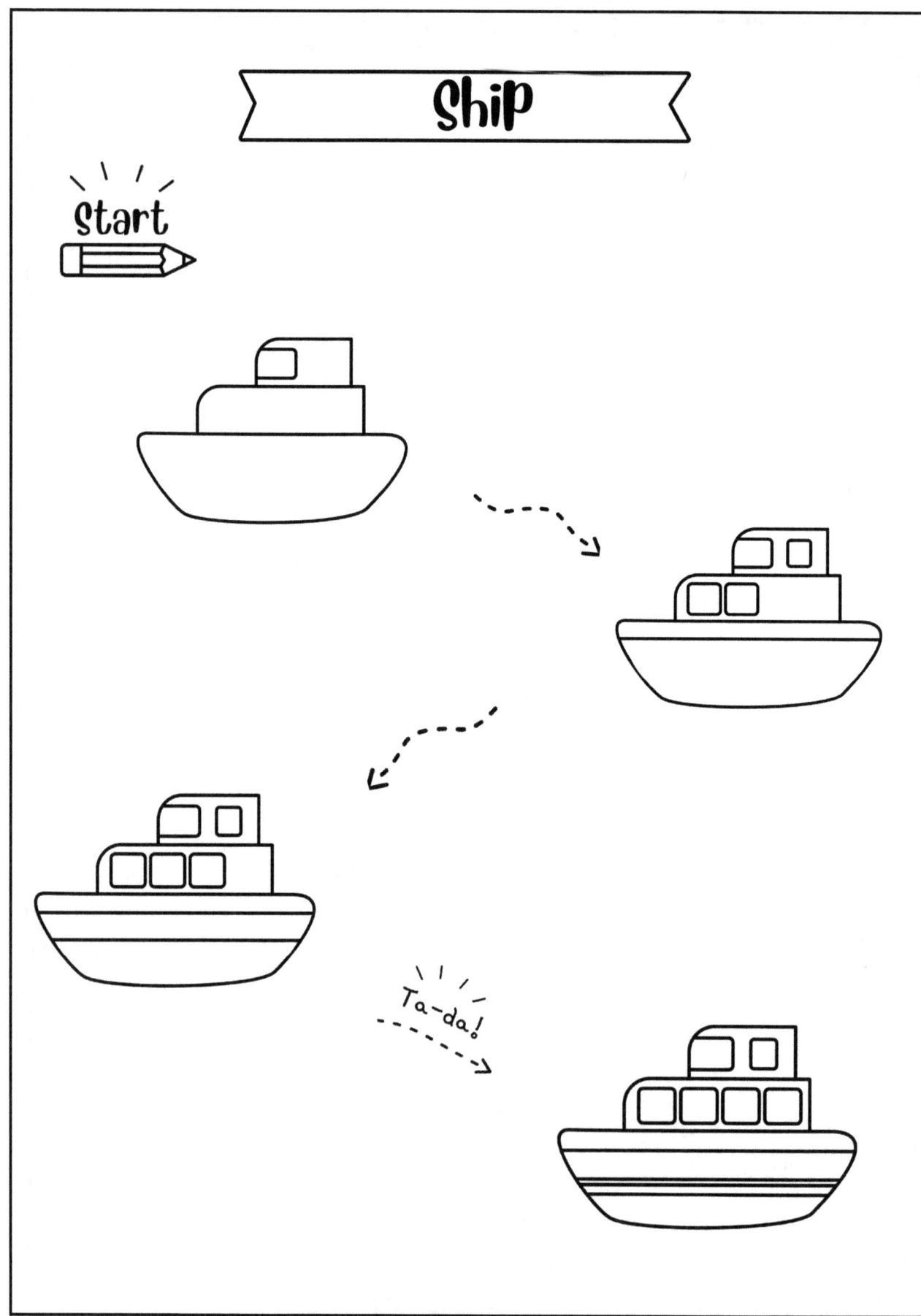

Your Drawing

Chicken

start

Ta-da!

Your Drawing

Car

Start

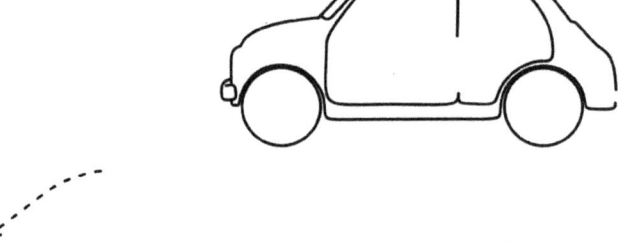

Ta-da!

Your Drawing

Submarine

Start

Ta-da!

Castle

Start

Ta-da!

Your Drawing

Rocket

Cute Cherries

Start

Ta-da!

Orange Tree

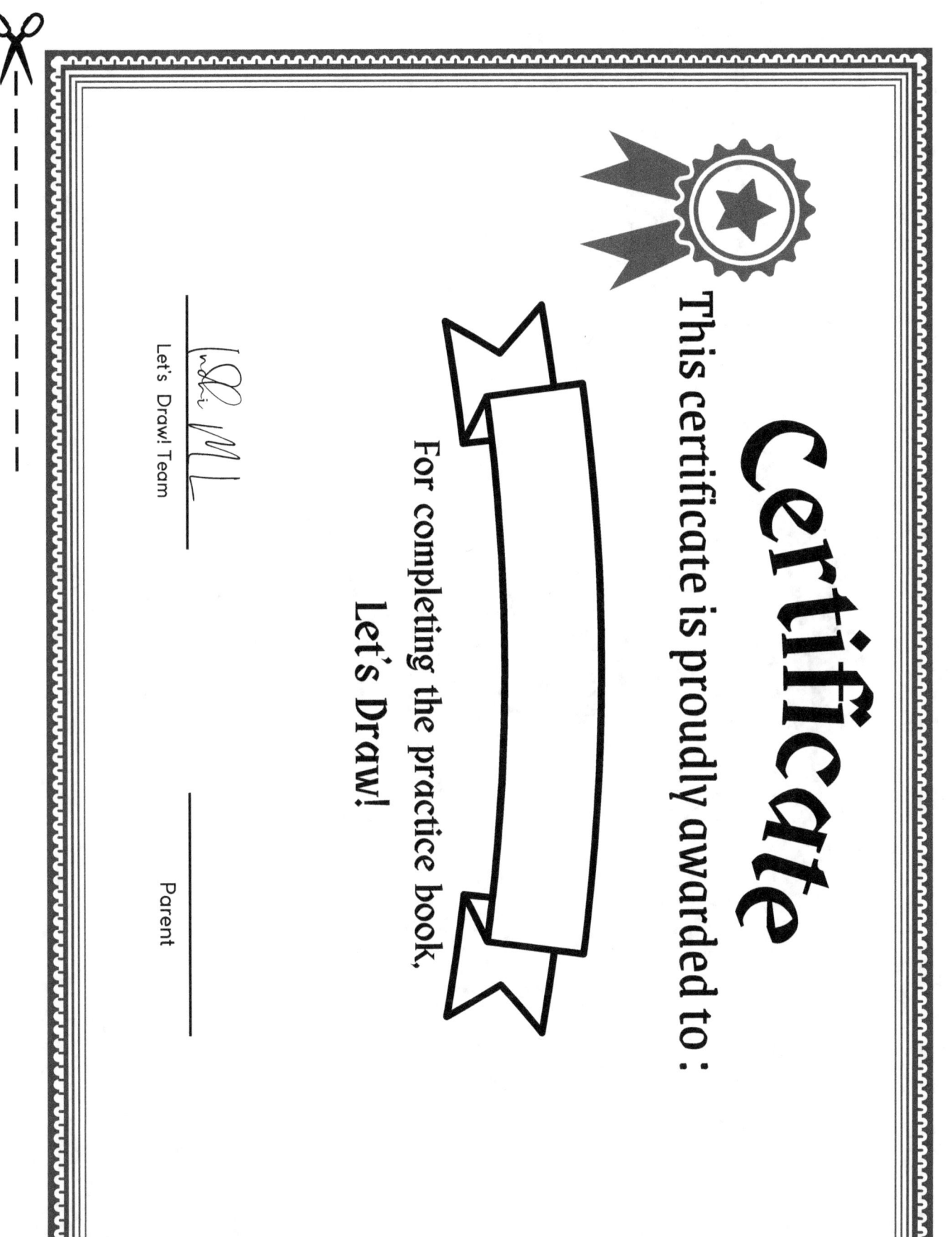

Well done!